Contents

The Secret War

Armed forces fought on land, at sea and in the air throughout the Second World War. But hidden from view were hundreds of men and women who fought a secret war — as code-breakers, undercover agents and resistance fighters.

War broke out in September 1939, when German forces invaded Poland, and Britain and France declared war on Germany. By 1941 the war, which lasted until 1945, was raging across the world. Each side struggled to gain the upper hand not only by fighting but also by gaining information.

> **"** We had an agreement with our man in Warsaw that he would let us know the moment hostilities started... I think it was when the first bomb dropped on Warsaw that he got through to us... and I had the signal brought in to me...**"**
>
> *Frederick Winterbotham, Secret Intelligence Service (SIS)*

Invasion

German troops and tanks roll into Poland on 1 September 1939 — the invasion that began the Second World War.

Secret War

Ann Kramer

W
FRANKLIN WATTS
LONDON•SYDNEY

IN ASSOCIATION WITH

IMPERIAL WAR

MUSEUM

This edition 2011

First published in 2010 by Franklin Watts

Copyright © 2010 Franklin Watts

Franklin Watts
338 Euston Road
London NW1 3BH

Franklin Watts Australia
Level 17/207 Kent Street
Sydney, NSW 2000

A CIP catalogue record for this book is available
from the British Library.

Dewey number: 940.5

ISBN 978 1 4451 0638 0

Printed in China

Franklin Watts is a division of Hachette Children's Books,
an Hachette UK company.

www.hachette.co.uk

Editor: Sarah Ridley
Design: Billin Design Solutions
Editor in Chief: John C. Miles
Art director: Jonathan Hair

With many thanks to Terry Charman and the staff at the Imperial
War Museum's Document, Sound and Photograph Archives.

Picture credits:

All images copyright © Imperial War Museum unless otherwise stated.

Front cover: HU 056936a, MH 027178, HU 016541, EA 033756, CL 003987
Back cover: HU 056936a, HU 053192, HU 036121, NA 025393, CL 003987
Insides: Title page CH 016680, p4 ©Ullsteinbild/TopFoto, p5 CH 016683, p6 PST 003750 IWM
repro right, p7 HU 036121, p8 Hulton Archive/Getty Images, p9 A 013709, p10 MH 0271178,
p11 MH 029100, p12 CH 016680, p13 CM 002450, p14 HU 053192, p15 ZZZ 011837,
p16 HU 016541, p17 HU 003213, p18 HU 056936a, p19 HU 060544, p20 Hulton Archive/Getty
Images, p21 HU 047367, p22 HU 061180, p23 HU 061185, p24 NA 025393, p25 CL 003987,
p26 HU 065147, p27 EA 033756, p28 HU 074868, p29 B 010081

A secret war

Secrecy was essential during the war so that each side did not know what the other was planning. Both sides used codes and ciphers to pass on sensitive military information such as plans of attack and numbers of weapons or troops. Getting this information was vital. In Britain thousands of men and women, in secret locations, intercepted enemy messages and decoded them, gathering information known as intelligence. They also put out false information to fool the enemy. Specially trained men and women risked their lives gathering intelligence and harassing the enemy in occupied territories.

New technology

Today, computers and CCTV cameras are part of everyday life. We are under constant surveillance and computerised databases hold information about all of us. We use email and mobile phones. In 1939 information technology was more basic. People wrote on paper and sent coded messages via telephones and wireless (radio) transmitters. Individuals spent hours and days puzzling out codes. As war progressed, new technology was developed, including computers.

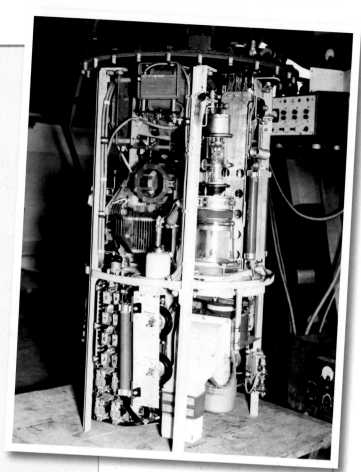

Jostling

Developed in secret, this piece of equipment was known as a 'jostle' transmitter. Attached to an aircraft, it was a jamming device, designed to disrupt enemy telephone communications.

“ The sort of person who volunteered [to be an agent] was in the main someone prepared to operate on their own with a considerable amount of courage and prepared to take considerable risks... ”

Vera Atkins, Special Operations Executive (SOE) HQ, London

Spy 'mania'

Fears about German spies swept through Britain from 1940. Government propaganda warned civilians not to gossip about the war and Germans and Italians living in Britain were rounded up.

"........ but for Heaven's sake don't say I told you!"

CARELESS TALK COSTS LIVES

Careless talk!

Eavesdropping Hitlers crowd around a telephone box in this poster, which warns of the dangers of 'careless talk'. It was designed by the British artist 'Fougasse' (Kenneth Bird).

British people were concerned the country was full of German spies. There were rumours that Germans were being parachuted into Britain, disguised as nuns. It was not true. There were some German spies and sympathisers in Britain but only a few and most were arrested. Some became double agents, working for Britain. But anxiety rose. Sometimes the Home Guard pounced on an innocent person because they believed he or she was behaving strangely and might be a spy.

Careless talk

In 1939, the British government began a 'Careless Talk Costs Lives' campaign telling people not to gossip about the war effort. Posters with slogans such as 'Walls Have Ears' and 'Be Like Dad, Keep Mum' appeared everywhere. Some posters were like cartoons. They showed ordinary people talking on buses or in restaurants, while Nazis such as Adolf Hitler eavesdropped on their conversation.

> **"** Suddenly, I was pounced on by two enormous men… They frisked me and looked in my pockets… They took me… to the police station. They were just enthusiastic Sandwich Local Defence people who thought they'd trapped a German descended on them by parachute… **"**
>
> *Francis Codd, auxiliary fireman, after being evacuated from Dunkirk back to Britain*

Internment

When war began the British government rounded up known Nazi sympathisers. In 1940, Italy entered the war on Germany's side. This led a few civilians to attack shops and restaurants owned by Germans or Italians. Between 1939-40, thousands of 'enemy aliens' were interned (detained) in bleak internment camps in Britain, or deported. It was a harsh policy that caused much distress. Many detainees had lived in Britain for years. Some were refugees fleeing Nazi persecution. From 1941, many internees were released.

Internment

Escorted by police, women classed as 'enemy aliens' board a train to be interned on the Isle of Man. Some internees were sent to Canada. However this policy was later changed due to public concern over the fairness of 'imprisoning' innocent people.

> **"** … there was my father, Luigi, my mother, sister… and two tall men in raincoats and trilby hats. They were policemen… My mother said, 'They've come to take Dad and Luigi away because Italy's come into the war…' My father said, '… I've been here since 1910. That's thirty years…' They took him [Luigi] away. **"**
>
> *Carmin Sidonio, wartime schoolboy, London*

Bletchley Park

One of the British government's best-kept secrets was Bletchley Park, a country house in Buckinghamshire that was code-named 'Station X'. During the war thousands of men and women worked around the clock at Bletchley Park, decoding secret enemy messages.

Station X began operations in 1939, when the British Government Code and Cipher School (GCCS) moved into the building from the Admiralty. In fact GCCS was not a school at all. It was a highly secret organisation, which was part of Britain's Secret Intelligence Service (SIS), now MI6. It played a vital role in Britain's secret war.

Bletchley Park

Bletchley Park, Buckinghamshire, was a grand country house before the war. It became the headquarters of the Allied effort to break the Nazis' secret codes.

> **"**... We were all sworn to secrecy... When the information came in cipher, you had to decode it. I became very quick at doing it... When the RAF came down to recruit people... I passed all the tests but was told I was too young... I was eventually taken on... that's how I found myself a WAAF under the age of eighteen... **"**

June Knowles (Watkins), Bletchley Park worker

Top secret

To start with there were only 150 people at Bletchley Park. As the volume of coded enemy intelligence increased, more people were needed. But because of its secret nature, they could not be recruited openly. Instead administrators approached potential recruits. Only certain people were suitable: they needed to be intelligent, thoughtful, adaptable and, above all, capable of keeping secrets. No one was allowed to talk about their work, not even to their family.

Busy traffic, 1942

Literally thousands of coded messages, known as 'traffic', flooded in and out of signals offices around Britain, and were passed onto Bletchley for decoding. Operators had to work fast and accurately. Mistakes could cost lives.

Growing numbers

In 1942, more than 3,000 people were working at Bletchley Park and by 1945, there were some 10,000. Some were civilians; others came from the armed forces. They included mathematicians, linguists, wireless operators and filing clerks. British, American, French and Polish people worked there. The original building could not hold everyone so wooden or concrete buildings known as 'huts' were built, each with its own number and purpose.

Cracking the code

Some of Britain's brainiest people worked at Bletchley Park. Their job was to crack the code used by Germany's Enigma machine.

All German armed forces used Enigma. It was a clever machine. Operators typed in plain letters and a series of rotating wheels, called rotors, scrambled the letters into code.

Remarkable people

Germany believed Enigma was unbreakable, but cryptanalysts (people who study codes) at Bletchley Park were determined that they could crack it. The team that worked on Enigma included some remarkable — and often eccentric — people. They were mathematicians, crossword enthusiasts, chess players and linguists. All of them had particular talents, such as maths and a love of word games, which are needed to unlock codes.

Enigma

The Enigma machine looked like an old-fashioned typewriter in a wooden box. An electrical current went from the keyboard through a set of rotors to light up the 'code' alphabet. Operators changed the settings every day.

Getting the clues

Polish code-breakers had begun to crack Enigma before the war. They passed the information onto Britain, and Bletchley Park continued the work. The machine could

encode in millions of ways, but it had flaws. It could not encipher a letter as itself, and German operators often used the same phrases. Armed with these clues, by 1940 the Bletchley team had broken the code. Settings changed daily but in 1941 an Enigma machine and its codebooks fell into British hands, after the capture of a German U-boat. Now they had much of the necessary information.

Bombes and Colossus

While code-breakers poured laboriously over codes, scientists and mathematicians, popularly known as 'boffins', developed new technology. Alan Turing, a brilliant mathematician, developed the Bombe, an early type of computer that could check codes faster than any human. In 1943, post office engineer Tommy Flowers and his team developed Colossus, the world's first programmable computer. It was the size of a room and extremely noisy but invaluable to the code-breakers.

Intercepting codes

More than 4,000 coded messages flooded into Bletchley Park every day. Information gathered was known as Ultra, for ultra secret. The secrets revealed helped the Allies to win the war.

Listening stations, known as Y stations, were dotted around Britain, and abroad. Telephonists and wireless operators worked night and day to intercept enemy messages. They transcribed them and forwarded them to Bletchley Park for decoding.

Working conditions

Operators at Bletchley worked eight-hour shifts around the clock, receiving and decoding messages. Most people worked in the huts, which were baking hot in summer and freezing cold in winter. Some operators sat at desks with headphones on, transcribing messages. Others sat in front of rows of dials on the huge Colossus and Bombe machines. The noise from these was overpowering.

Operation Dartboard

Codes were used to try and confuse the enemy as well. This equipment was used by German-speaking Royal Air Force personnel to transmit orders to enemy aircraft on their own wave length, code-named Operation Dartboard.

> **"** I think the most important signal we had decrypted through Ultra right at the beginning of the Battle of Britain, was Goering establishing his strategy with his commanders. He told them that they were to fly over Britain and bring the whole of the Royal Air Force up to battle... that was the key to fight the battle with very small units... **"**
>
> *Frederick Winterbotham, Secret Intelligence Service*

Part of a chain

Individuals often only saw part of any message. They did the work in front of them, and then passed it onto the next person. Sometimes they never knew the final message, although word often went round when something valuable had been decoded, such as Germany's plans for bombing Britain.

Golden eggs

Ultra — information gathered from Enigma — was invaluable. It helped the Allies to plan strategy for the Battle of Britain, fight U-boats in the Atlantic and plan campaigns in North Africa. Prime Minister Winston Churchill called Ultra his 'golden eggs'. He once said that the 'geese' that laid the golden eggs — the staff at Bletchley — 'never cackled'. He was right. Colossus and the Bombes were dismantled after the war and information about Bletchley Park was not made public until the 1970s.

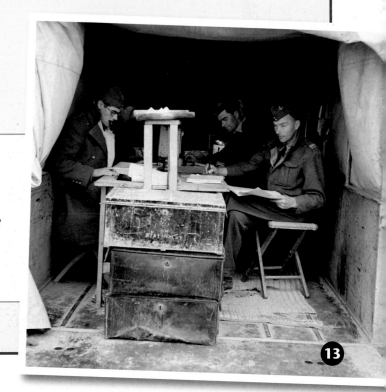

Mobile ciphering, 1942

RAF cipher officers work in a mobile cipher van in the Western Desert, North Africa. Intercepting coded messages and deciphering them meant the Allies could gain valuable information about enemy movements. Similarly Allied commanders coded their messages.

SOE

Between 1939-40, German forces swept through Poland, Norway, Denmark, Holland, Belgium and France. They seemed invincible. British Prime Minister Winston Churchill ordered the formation of a secret volunteer organisation called the Special Operations Executive, or SOE.

A few British agents were already operating undercover. They were trying to organise resistance to hinder the Axis advance but without much success.

Setting Europe ablaze

In July 1940, SOE was set up with orders from Churchill to "set Europe ablaze". To do so SOE would send agents into occupied Europe to carry out sabotage, spy on the enemy and help resistance movements. It would be very dangerous. Any agent captured by the Germans could expect to be tortured and executed.

Wheelwright

George Starr, code-named 'Hilaire', was one of SOE's most successful agents. He arrived in France in 1942, where he posed as a retired Belgian mining engineer. He ran a group, code-named 'Wheelwright', which spied on the Germans and helped to liberate Toulouse in 1944.

> 66 We were totally amateurish… You can't suddenly create an effective organisation with the aims that SOE had… to support resistance and promote resistance in countries that might be occupied and, when they were occupied, to keep the links going… Very difficult… 99
>
> *Basil Davidson, Section D and SOE officer, Hungary*

London headquarters

SOE made its headquarters at 64 Baker Street, London, not far from where the famous but fictitious Sherlock Holmes was supposed to have lived. Its first head was a Labour politician, Hugh Dalton. Older secret service organisations, such as MI6, were not keen on SOE because they thought it was amateurish and sabotage tactics would cause unwanted German attention. But SOE went ahead, started recruiting and gained experience.

Brave individuals

At its peak 13,000 men and women worked for SOE. Five thousand were agents. They included immensely brave individuals. Agents operated not just in Europe, but also Burma, North Africa and the Middle East. Most were British but there were also Americans, Dutch, Norwegians, Poles, French and Jewish German and Austrian agents.

Sabotage, 1944

The SOE used sabotage extensively to harass the enemy. SOE agents and French resistance fighters blew up this railway depot. Agents also blew up bridges and railway lines, causing considerable disruption to the enemy.

"I was invited, aged just over twenty-one, to start a revolution in Albania against the Italians and given a budget of about £50,000 to get on with it... I collected some refugees. The next thing was to run lines of communication into Albania. That meant smuggling agents across the border...

Julian Amery, Section D and SOE officer, Yugoslavia

15

Recruitment

As the Blitz raged over London, SOE started recruiting. They needed agents who had the courage and skills to operate behind enemy lines. And they needed staff to run the organisation and liaise with agents.

Finding the right recruits was not simple. SOE had to be kept secret so recruitment was done discretely. Existing SOE people approached individuals they already knew — the 'old boys' network' — but as time went on the recruiting net was cast wider.

Recruits

SOE recruited men and women. Some came from the armed forces; others were civilians. Many were wealthy but recruits also came from more varied backgrounds. Agents included academics, journalists, military personnel and a former chef.

Executed

Violette Szabo was half-French, and a courageous woman. She joined the FANYs after her husband was killed fighting with the Free French, and was recruited by SOE. She was sent to France but was captured after a shoot-out with German soldiers. She was tortured and shot at Ravensbrück concentration camp. She was awarded the George Cross — Britain's highest civilian award for gallantry.

One SOE agent, Violette Szabo, was the daughter of a London car dealer. Several women were recruited from the FANYs — the First Aid Nursing Yeomanry, a rather select group.

Unknown work

Most recruits had no idea what work they would be doing. A woman called Elizabeth Small, for instance, wanted to join the WRNS but was sent to SOE because she had good secretarial skills and spoke French. At interview she was only told her work would be 'interesting'. SOE disguised itself under different names. Recruits often arrived for interview thinking they would be working for a government economic ministry, or a special research unit.

A big organisation

By 1944, thousands of people were involved with SOE in a whole range of jobs: they included secretaries, dispatch riders, trainers, explosives experts, engineers, wireless operators, administrators — and agents.

Odette Sansom, 1946

SOE sent Odette Sansom into occupied France as a courier in 1942. The Germans captured her and another agent, Peter Churchill, in 1943. They pretended they were married and related to Winston Churchill, which saved their lives. They were tortured but survived. She was also awarded the George Cross.

Training

Would-be agents were carefully checked for suitability. If accepted, they had to undergo a gruelling period of training before being sent into enemy territory.

Most agents were interviewed three times. Experienced recruiting officers grilled them to assess their character, skills, loyalty and reasons for wanting to be agents. Agents were vetted for security, and then finally told the nature of the work and its dangers. At this point they were asked if they wanted to continue: most did.

Commando-style

Training began in England, often at stately homes taken over by SOE. From there agents were sent on commando-style courses. They went on route marches and were taught how to use guns and explosives. They learned techniques of unarmed combat, and how to creep up on an enemy and kill him silently with a knife.

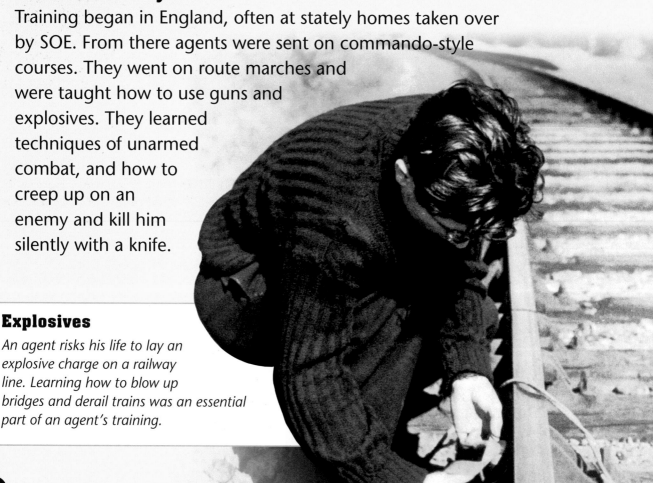

Explosives

An agent risks his life to lay an explosive charge on a railway line. Learning how to blow up bridges and derail trains was an essential part of an agent's training.

Sabotage techniques

Explosives experts showed agents how to lay charges and blow up bridges, trains and railway lines. In Scotland, agents practised with dummy explosives, laying them secretly under trains and bridges. Trainees also learned more advanced industrial sabotage in order to detonate pylons and factories.

Risky missions, 1943

Lysander aircraft such as this flew agents and supplies into Nazi-occupied France. The pilot, Flying Officer J A McCairns (middle), flew several secret missions.

Survival and communications

Trainee agents needed to know how to survive in enemy territory. Training exercises included being dropped in unfamiliar places then having to get home; how to follow someone or lose a follower; and how to survive interrogation. Agents were taught how to use wireless transmitters and code messages. Trainees also learned how to parachute out of a plane, which could be terrifying for someone who had never done it before.

Fake identities

SOE agents were given cover stories or false identities before going into enemy-occupied territory. They had to know them perfectly. Planning needed to be meticulous: small mistakes could blow an agent's cover.

It was risky being in Nazi-occupied Europe. Police and Gestapo were everywhere, and anything suspicious could be reported to the authorities. Agents passed themselves off as artists, farmers, salesmen or ordinary citizens. Some spoke foreign languages fluently; others did not. SOE provided clothes and forged papers.

Fearsome sight
German soldiers patrol the streets somewhere in the Netherlands, autumn 1944.

Small details

London briefed agents thoroughly but sometimes details were missed. One agent's cover was blown when he went into a French café and ordered a black coffee. He was noticed because he did not know milk was rationed and only black coffee was available. Another agent arrived in France wearing English leather shoes. A Frenchwoman noticed this because no one in France could buy leather.

> **"**My cover story was that I'd been a fashion artist... in Paris just before the war. Being an artist... you can go anywhere... You could walk around with your paintbox and do little sketches of the countryside... And... the transmitters were fairly small, so mine was built into a box of paints...**"**
>
> *Lieutenant Brian Stonehouse, SOE wireless operator, France*

Suitable work for women

At first SOE only used men as undercover agents. Women made passports, ration cards, identity papers and other forged documents. Some, such as Vera Atkins, prepared agents for going into France. From 1942, Churchill gave permission for women to be sent into the field. Many people thought women could move around much more easily than men, and were far less noticeable. Once in the field SOE set up networks, known as circuits. Three members of a circuit were particularly important: the organiser, the courier and the wireless operator. Circuit leaders tended to be men. Female agents worked as wireless operators and couriers, who needed to be constantly on the move.

> "Everything had to look authentic... If there was a man going out dressed as a bargee his clothes had to look like a bargee's clothes... we had to rub it down or do darns, make a hole and tear it... and darn it roughly, so it would look old..."
>
> *May Shrubb, technician, The Thatched Barn, Hertfordshire (see page 22)*

Tools of the trade

Agents carried a lot of equipment, from explosives through to maps and radios. Backroom technicians invented ingenious ways of producing and disguising the tools agents needed.

Explosive bricks

These hollowed-out bricks hid explosives and ammunition. At a quick glance, they look just like normal bricks. The SOE used all sorts of everyday objects to hide explosives, including dead mice.

Technicians worked in secret locations. One was The Frythe, a secluded house in Hertfordshire, where devices such as a single-shot cigarette pistol were developed. Another was The Thatched Barn, where SOE's camouflage section invented such things as exploding horse manure.

"They used to develop all sorts of things… the Welbike, a collapsible motorbike [that] folded up and went into a parachute container… Triangular nails which agents… used to… puncture tyres… And explosive turds… Lumps of manure that blew up when you ran over them…"

Captain Peter Lee, Security Section Officer, SOE HQ, London

Weapons

Saboteurs needed timed fuses and detonators so they could get away before an explosion. One development was the time pencil, a tiny detonator. Pressing a ridge on the pencil produced an acid, which ate through wire, releasing a spring. The detonator exploded and the bomb went up. Some saboteurs carried sub-machine guns that arrived in three sections, with simple assembly instructions.

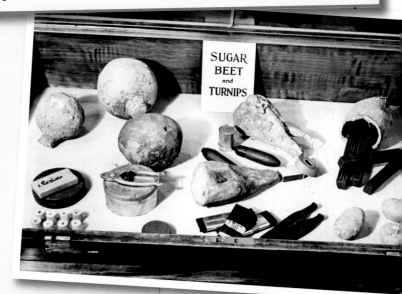

Wireless radio transmitter

A wireless was an essential piece of equipment. British agents used suitcase radios to send and receive coded messages. They were heavy and bulky. The wireless weighed about 13.6 kg (30 lbs) and fitted into a 60.9 cm (2 ft) long suitcase. As war progressed, smaller radios were developed.

Fake vegetables

Looking like ordinary sugarbeet and turnips, these fake vegetables were used to hide the various pieces of spy equipment lying around them.

Hidden objects and suicide pills

Agents carried maps, papers and compasses in hollowed out shoe heels, handbag linings, or even the stem of a pipe. They used invisible ink for messages. Tiny cameras were disguised as matchboxes, and paper-thin maps were stuck to playing cards. In case of capture or torture SOE agents carried suicide pills hidden in clothes or jewellery.

Parachuting in

Once trained, agents were ready to go. Getting in and out of occupied territory was difficult. Some were taken by sea but most parachuted in or landed by aircraft.

Before leaving England, agents had a final briefing. Papers and clothes were checked and SOE gave them a final gift, something valuable like a silver cigarette case, that they could use as a bribe.

Moonlight flights

SOE used RAF pilots for 'special missions' — flying agents and supplies into enemy territory. Flights were at night, around the time of the full moon. Agents arrived with their cases, nervous, excited or very quiet. Pilots took off. As they approached a pre-arranged dropping off point, agents pushed themselves out and parachuted down. Sometimes pilots landed briefly to drop off an agent or collect another for de-briefing in London.

Helping partisans, 1945

Essential supplies float down to resistance fighters in northern Italy. British pilots flew special missions to drop weapons, ammunition, radios and food to partisans and guerrilla fighters throughout mainland Europe.

" … we jumped… I slid down the side of a tree into a bunch of cows. We were welcomed… but… the chateau where we were supposed to spend the rest of the night had been raided by French police, so we had to leave the area as soon as possible…"

Lieutenant Brian Stonehouse, SOE wireless operator, France

Dropping zone, 1944

Parachutes and containers dropped by pilots of RAF Bomber Command litter a dropping zone in Belgium. If all went well, agents and resisters collected them but sometimes there was a tip-off and when resisters arrived, they were arrested.

Reception committees

The first agents to go into the field dropped 'blind' with no one to meet them. They had to find trustworthy locals, safe houses and establish contact with local resistance groups. Later, 'reception committees' of local resisters met incoming agents at the drop off. They shone lights to guide aircraft, hid parachutes and helped agents on their way. It was risky. Locals faced arrest if found out after curfew.

> " ... As soon as I entered this restaurant whom should I see but two blokes from SOE... according to our training, I went in front of the table, dropped my newspaper... picked it up, looked him in the eye... and I went to the next room... He followed... and put me in touch with the organisation..."
>
> *Captain Robert Boiteux, SOE circuit organiser, France*

Set backs

Missions were planned carefully but problems arose. Bad weather meant a flight was cancelled or delayed, which was nerve-wracking for stressed out agents. Some agents parachuted off course, into trees or rocks. Sometimes missions were betrayed and agents arrived to find the enemy waiting for them.

Fighting behind enemy lines

From 1942, SOE agents were operating behind enemy lines throughout Nazi-occupied Europe. Together with partisans and resistance groups, they waged a formidable secret war against the enemy.

SOE sent out its first agents in 1941. They established extensive networks and worked with resistance men and women in different areas. Agents trained them, provided arms and helped to organise missions.

Sabotage and assassination

SOE's aim was to sabotage the enemy on every front. They took enormous risks. In 1942, agents led Greek guerrilla forces in a daring assault on the Gorgopotamos viaduct and blew it up. The following year a nine-man team of British-trained Norwegian commandos braved the mountains to blow up the Norsk heavy-water plant at Vermork, ending Hitler's plans for an atomic bomb. And in 1942, two

Albania

In 1943 SOE parachuted a team into Albania led by Major Billy McLean, shown here shaking hands with partisan Xhelai Staravecke. McLean's team trained and armed the partisans.

" ...Major Scott attached a piece of safety fuse to the explosive charges and waited till we heard the train approaching and at the last minute lit the fuse and ran... The explosives went off just under his [driver's] engine, derailed it and tipped it over...**"**

Sergeant Ray Mason, SOE wireless operator, Greece

> **"**… we cut all the railway lines, we cut all the communication lines, telephone lines and we blew up a lot of bridges, electric transformers, so that no Germans were able to leave Bordeaux and the district there and reinforce the Normandy beaches.**"**
>
> *Major Roger Landes, SOE circuit organiser, France*

SOE-trained Czech agents assassinated Reinhard Heydrich, a hated Nazi commander. There were dreadful reprisals: the Nazis murdered over 5,000 Czech men, women and children in revenge.

French Resistance

SOE sent more agents into France than anywhere else. Working closely with the French Resistance, they harried the enemy constantly, blowing up railway lines, pylons and conducting a guerrilla war against the Nazis. In 1941, SOE agents and resisters blew up Pessac power station, bringing railways to a halt. By 1944, SOE had built up a secret army of some 10,000 French men and women. They sabotaged German communication systems, paving the way for the D-Day Allied landings, and hampered the movement of German troops attempting to get to Normandy.

Armed resistance

A heavily armed member of the French Resistance poses with his Bren gun. SOE sent more than 1,000 agents to France and eventually provided half a million arms for the French resistance.

Capture

Agents in the field lived with the fear of capture or betrayal. If captured, they were treated as spies and executed. About 200 agents lost their lives.

Noor Inayat Khan

Code-named 'Madeleine', Noor Inayat Khan was SOE's first woman wireless operator to be sent to France. She arrived in 1943. Other agents in her circuit were arrested but she continued sending messages to England. She was betrayed, arrested and tortured but gave nothing to the Gestapo. In 1944, she was executed at Dachau concentration camp with three other women agents — Madeleine Damerment, Elaine Plewman and Yolande Beekman. She was awarded the George Cross (see page 16).

SOE agents used every precaution to avoid being detected. They used special signals and passwords and kept on the move. They changed safe houses and hid out with resistance workers. Some agents had very narrow escapes.

Betrayal

Agents were betrayed, particularly in France. One circuit, known as 'Prosper', was destroyed when an apparently trustworthy

> **"** … I was stopped by some gendarmes… They asked for my identity card… they said, 'What have you got in your sacoches [saddlebags]?' … I said… just a few night things… and… pulled out a towel. The explosives were in the bottom… my leg started shaking… one said, 'Are you cold?' I said yes… He said 'OK, go on.' **"**
>
> *Lieutenant Harry Rée, SOE circuit organiser, France*

agent turned out to be a double agent. His information led to the capture of many SOE agents. Germans captured an agent in Holland, and forced him to keep sending messages to London. The agent used pre-arranged codes to tell London that he had been captured but they were ignored. More agents were sent out. Dozens were captured.

Vulnerable

Wireless operators were particularly vulnerable. They were responsible for sending messages to London and receiving instructions. Putting messages into code was a lengthy process and German detector vans could track wireless signals within 30 minutes. On average, wireless operators lasted only six weeks in France.

Grim prospect

This picture shows a cell — with shackles attached to the wall — at the Gestapo interrogation centre at Breedonck in Belgium. Captured agents were tortured in cells such as this.

Capture

Once captured, agents were interrogated, often very brutally. Some cracked and revealed information. Others remained silent. Several were taken to concentration camps and executed. Some survived and returned after the war.

Glossary

Allies Britain and Commonwealth countries, the Soviet Union (USSR), France and the USA, which fought against the Axis Powers.

Axis Powers Germany, Italy, Japan and some other Eastern European countries, which fought against the Allies.

Bargee A person who operates a barge.

Churchill, Winston British prime minister 1940-45.

Ciphers These use single letters, which may be jumbled up or replaced by other letters, numbers or symbols.

Circuit Name given to SOE networks.

Codes These are based on complete words and phrases. Words are replaced by code words or numbers.

Curfew An order made by occupying forces that people had to remain indoors after a certain time in the evening.

Encipher To put a message into code.

Enemy aliens Foreigners living in Britain who were citizens of countries at war with Britain, particularly Germany and Italy.

Gestapo German secret police.

Goering, Hermann The Commander in Chief of the German Luftwaffe (air force) and designated successor to Adolf Hitler.

Guerrilla Underground fighter, member of an independent fighting group, often working undercover.

Hitler, Adolf Austrian-born dictator of Germany and leader of the National Socialist (Nazi) Party 1933-45.

Jamming Disrupting or interfering with radio communications.

Linguist Someone who is good at languages.

Nazi Short for National Socialist — an extreme right-wing political party led by Adolf Hitler. It controlled Germany from 1933-1945.

Occupied territories Lands or countries under the control of Nazi Germany.

Partisan Member of an armed resistance group fighting against an occupying power.

Propaganda Information put out by the government through the radio, leaflets and posters that influences what people do.

Resisters Resistance fighters who are members of resistance groups fighting secretly against occupying powers.

Safe house A house where agents in danger could hide or meet secretly.

Second World War (1939-45) Also known as World War II. Fought between the Axis Powers, which included Germany, Italy and Japan and the Allies, which included Britain, Commonwealth countries, France, Russia and the USA.

SOE Special Operations Executive.

Further information
Books

My Second World War, Daniel James, Franklin Watts in association with the Imperial War Museum, 2008

Posters and Propaganda in Wartime, Daniel James and Ruth Thomson, Franklin Watts in association with the Imperial War Museum, 2007

The Second World War, Dennis Hamley, Franklin Watts, 2007

Some useful websites

http://london.iwm.org.uk
The Imperial War Museum has lots of information on Enigma and the code-breakers. It also has a permanent exhibition about the work of agents and others working with Special Operations Executive. It includes spy equipment and information about agents.

http://www.codesandciphers.org.uk/bletchleypark/index.htm
A virtual tour of Bletchley Park with information about Enigma and the code-breakers.

http://www.bletchleypark.org.uk/content/machines.rhtm
Photos and information about the machines used by the code-breakers at Bletchley Park.

http://www.64-baker-street.org/main/index.html
The amazing stories of women agents who served with the Special Operations Executive.

Note to parents and teachers:
Every effort has been made by the Publishers to ensure that the websites in this book are suitable for children, that they are of the highest educational value, and that they contain no inappropriate or offensive material. However, because of the nature of the Internet, it is impossible to guarantee that the contents of these sites will not be altered. We strongly advise that Internet access is supervised by a responsible adult.

Index